Creativity: Developing, Nurturing

Creativity—we all had it once. But somewhere between our youth and the present, it may have been lost in the serious process of growing up and conforming. It need not be gone forever, though.

To re-develop our innate creativity, we must regain our childlike daring, independence, and unconventional sense of humor. We must be willing once again to risk, to experiment, to attempt the somewhat absurd, to be flexible, non-conforming, and curious. We must re-develop our courage and self-confidence, and above all, our ability to risk, when its so much easier to be content just conforming the "the rules." Why try to re-ignite a stiffled creativity. Indeed, **why not?!**

Re-kindling and nurturing individual creativity requires an environment which, in the beginning at least, is sufficiently structured to provide a sense of security and support while simultaneously encouraging experimentation, daring, risk taking, and even the making of mistakes. A supportive atmosphere (one which recognizes that making mistakes and learning from them is a vital part of the creative process) makes openness and receptivity possible, and it minimizes the fear of failure which hampers the daring to create.

It is this gentle, supportive structuring, combined with strong encouragement, which is the basis of my Freehanding Seminars and which I hope to provide in this book by offering just enough guidance to nudge you into experimenting. I have found it necessary in the teaching of creativity to avoid stepping in too soon to help bail a student out of a stymieing freehand designing exercise. To interfere before the student has had a chance to attempt to work through experiments on his or her own deprives that student of the opportunity to err and then profit from that error. **So much creative activity and learning takes place in attempting to work one's way out of a bind. Fresh ideas, valuable insights, and new approaches develop.**

In trying to direct students into creative behavior, I encourage them to tackle large painting projects in small bits at a ti[me ...] reinforcements a[nd ...] carry on. Our first freehand designing object is a circular piece on which we develop a geometric design. The geometric design allows us to decorate even a 24" tilt top table quite successfully by making one decision at a time and acting on each one before going on to the next. The geometric design, of course, because of its repetitive nature, provides a structured environment which allows for a safe amount of experimenting. By the time the student has acted on a single decision for 8, 12, 16 repetitions around the circular piece, more and more confidence is developed—definitely positive reinforcement. And so the creative experience becomes a little less fearsome. By the time it's necessary to make a new creative decision in order to develop the next phase of the design, it's a little easier. After several such decisions and positive reinforcements, the design begins to take shape.

The purpose of the geometric design, like the seminar and this book, is to impose just enough structuring to provide a secure atmosphere, but at the same time not so much that creativity is hemmed in. Frequently, on the book's design worksheets, many possibilities are given; and where no choices are deliberately offered, it is hoped that you will begin to think with flexibility to create your own. For instance, if something is right side up, consider how it would look upside down, or—

inside out, backwards, sideways, in silhouette, in another color, in two or more colors, with curves squared off, with corners rounded, in a straight line, in a curvy line, repeated in a mirror image, larger, smaller, one inside another, with details, without details, bold, delicate, dark, light, combined with something else, framed, unframed, realistic, primitive, fancy, plain.

How many more variations can you conjure up? Think: **if this, why not that?** Open yourself up to fresh, flexible thinking. It will serve you—and your decorative painting—well.

Avoiding Frustration

In freehand designing and stroke painting there is a tendency to be discouraged at first, particularly before the embellishing is complete. Don't give in to frustration. Push on. Just be aware that if you do feel frustrated, you're quite normal. It's all a part of the growing process. Whatever you create, try to make something out of it. To give up and wipe it out (whether it be a single stroke, a nearly completed flower, or an entire design) represents two steps backward. Not only does it slow you down, but it also impedes your creativity. Creative impulses and impetus are deterred by concentrating on the negative. Think positively, acceptingly, and have enough faith in yourself to know that you **can** do it, and that you **can** make the best of whatever happens.

It's time to toss timidity away. Approach your free-handing with a flair and a fresh, lively attitude. Do not agonize over trying to create the perfect design for a piece. Instead, just sit down and paint on it. Let whatever happens happen. Day by day, and experience by experience, you will come to know what pleases you and

what does not. You will reinforce the positive experiences and eliminate the negative ones from future painting. Soon enough, your "perfect designs" will begin to emerge quite naturally along with your own unique style. Just be patient with yourself.

Whenever you're feeling down on your own technique or talent, immerse yourself in resource books from the library on all the different folk arts from other countries. Years of delving into old books—many in languages I could not read—has been a great inspiration to me. Books on metal and tinsmithing, woodworking, needleworks, church and temple arts, manuscript illumination, as well as books illustrating the life styles and fads of different eras all contain fascinating inspirations. What you will discover in the old folk arts is an expression of delight, complete with all the idiosyncracies, the imperfections, the rough edges—and above all, the charm of a creation made for the sheer love of doing it. And isn't that what decorative painting is all about!

Getting Started in Freehand Designing

Once you have mastered the basic strokes and have begun creating interesting stroke combinations, then it is time to begin thinking about creating your own unique designs.

Although space here doesn't allow for the kind of emphasis I like to place on design in my seminars, I do want to share a few hints with you. They are abbreviated, but they should at least help focus your thinking.

1. Select a color scheme. Use aids such as wallpaper and fabric scraps—things which already have color combinations pleasing to you. Test the colors selected for compatibility with your background color by putting them on a piece of clear acetate. Place the acetate against your prepared project to see how well the selected colors coordinate with the background.

2. Study the project (i.e. a large rocking horse). Think of it in terms of its parts (i.e. head, saddle, legs, rockers . . .). Do not let the entire project overwhelm you. Break it down mentally, into sections. Concentrate on only one section at a time (i.e. saddle). That section, then, may also be divided into sections using bands of contrasting colors, ovals, or circles, thereby making an even less intimidating area to decorate.

3. Develop a theme (i.e. roses, daisies, strokes, dots. . .). Repeat this central theme throughout the entire project. This will help pull all the individual parts together unifying them as parts of the whole. Repeat colors, strokes, and designs for balance as well as coordination.

4. Divide with chalk those areas to be decorated. Use the chalk minimally to sketch guide lines, and areas to hold spaces for flowers and other design elements. Avoid sketching entire designs as to do so will be too confining. Sketch only what you absolutely need.

5. Use surface texturizing techniques—such as those illustrated on the back cover to add interest and variety to projects.

Supplies Needed

Brushes-
Loew-Cornell
Series 7300 #2,4,8,12 (optional #6,10)
Series 7550 1/2"
Series 7000 #4 round
Jackie's Liner JS #2

Note: The above brushes (less optional #6 and 10) are available in handy kit form with molded plastic carrying case. Ask for **Jackie Shaw's Decorative Folk Art Brush Kit** by Loew-Cornell at your favorite art and craft supply store. Or write Decorative Design Studio, Box 155, Smithsburg, MD 21783 for ordering information.

Paints—Acrylics, oils or watercolors. The illustrations throughout this book were done with Folk Art Acrylics by Plaid Enterprises.

Palette paper—Such as 4-in-1 Disposable Palette by Aquabee

Parchment paper—Such as Calligraphic Parchment Paper by Bienfang. Parchment is ideal for practicing strokes and designs as it is sturdier and more durable than tracing paper. (If working with oils, lightly spray the paper with an acrylic spray or a sealer to prevent an oil "halo" around painting.)

Mastering Brush Control

Assuming you bought this book because you seriously want help in improving and developing your strokework and freehanding style, I'm going to share with you a number of hints for working with your brushes. It's one thing to read through them and think, "Hmmm, that's interesting;" but the hints will do you no good unless you pay close attention and actually put them into practice.

1. As a brush stroke artist, particularly a freehanding one, you have two vitally important tools: your brush and—of all things—your shoulder. To try to use your brush without also using your shoulder is about as futile as trying to use a sewing machine without electricity. The machine **can** be cranked by hand, but what a jerky, awkward, and tiring way to sew. How much smoother, surer, and more flowing the stitchery would be if only you'd plug in the machine and take advantage of the power source. The same thing is true in painting. You **can** crank out the brush strokes by hand—a laborious and often jerky process; or you can engage the "power source" and let the strokes flow smoothly and rhythmically from your shoulder. Until you've mastered the freedom of working with your shoulder and entire arm

(rather than with only brush and fingers) you cannot appreciate what a vast difference this can make in your stroke painting. **Of all the hints I will be sharing with you throughout this book, this one, without a doubt, will make the greatest difference in helping you master brush control and develop your own freehanding skill and spontaneous style.**

2. Sit comfortably. Ideally, you should work at a low table, or on a high stool, or in your lap so that your entire arm is free to move. If you are having to hitch your shoulder up in order to paint on a table. you are **not** comfortable (as you'll soon discover via a pain across your back, neck, or shoulder).

3. With your arm hanging freely from your shoulder, keep your wrist, forearm, and elbow off the table! No resting on anything except your little finger—and that **should never be stationary.** It must move freely as an extension of your arm, all moving as a single unit. The little finger may be extended or curved under, whichever way you find most comfortable (both ways will seem awkward initially, so just keep working on it). The little

finger serves as a pivot, a support for your arm, and a lever helping you to control thick/thin pressure and release on strokes. Use it to advantage.

4. Hold the brush **perpendicular** to your painting surface. This gives you the greatest control, easily permitting you to apply and release pressure for thick/thin strokes, and to allow brush hairs to begin on knife edge, or point, and return to same at the completion of the stroke. Avoid holding the brush as you would a pen or pencil—laid back and relaxed in your hand.

5. Load the brush thoroughly. A couple of quick dabs in the paint puddle is **not** thorough. Apply pressure in loading paint into the brush by stroking firmly through the paint, permitting the brush to grab the paint and hold as much in its hairs as possible without globs clinging to the edges. So many difficulties in mastering brush control can be eliminated with proper loading techniques.

6. Paint will need to be thinned to a smoothly flowing consistency for many liner and sideloaded strokes. Use it thicker for detail strokes and areas where texture is desired.

7. Practice strokes very large and very small. Push your brush to extremes. You should be able to form a flat brush stroke which is double the width of the brush. Likewise, with your liner, practice making the largest stroke possible, then the tiniest one. Such practice helps you develop control. Practice the strokes in all directions.

8. Stay in control of the brush at all times.

a. Near the ends of strokes, slow down to permit hairs to return to natural formation (chisel edge for flat,

point for round or liner). Come to a complete stop. Then lift off. Rarely is a stroke to be completed in mid air—that is, lifting off before letting hairs return to chisel or point, and before a complete stop.

b. Let the handle **pull** the hairs of the brush. Rarely should you **push** the hairs with the handle (the few exceptions will be noted on stroke pages which follow). Experiment with pushing and pulling the hairs to see why this procedure is so important.

c. Lean into the curves. Let your brush handle lean around curves just as you would on a bicycle. This helps permit the hairs to **follow** the handle.

9. Develop a flowing rhythm of pressure and release, always thinking contrast, **CONTRAST**! Create exciting artistic and visual impact with variations in thick and thin, long and short, nearly straight and very curvy. Be expressive. Give your brush work some punch, some flair, some style that says, "I did it; I'm glad I did it; and I loved doing it"!!

10. Paint confidently and with authority. Put strokes down and leave them alone. Whatever may happen at the end of your brush, reject the temptation to try to paint over it, to improve it. To do so almost always results in a situation worse than the original stroke. Leave it alone, and though others may not understand it, at least, they will assume you meant it since you left it there.

11. Practice! Great pianists practice daily, great skaters skate daily, great runners rún daily, great painters paint daily. Get the picture? Be patient with yourself and remember that (according to poet Piet Hein) TTT—"Things take time."

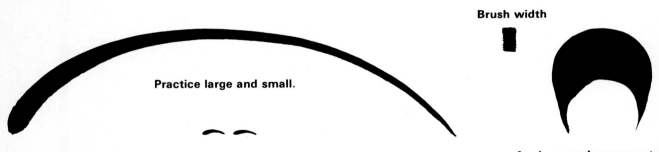

Brush width

Practice large and small.

Apply enough pressure to double the width of the brush.

Using the stroke worksheets

Study the strokes on pages 7–12 carefully; much of your understanding of what is developed further on in the book will depend upon your mastery of these strokes. The arrows on the strokes are there to give you a point of reference in the beginning. Ultimately, you will want to be able to paint all strokes in all directions. It's really easier that way than having to turn a large hutch or a wall (!) upside down or stand on your head because you can only paint in one direction.

On many of the stroke combination worksheets, you will notice a "key" located in the upper right hand corner advising "Look For These Strokes." The basic **flat brush** strokes used on that page will be illustrated in the

key. The actual strokes in the designs may be larger, smaller, upside down, sideways, twisted a little, or in some other way slightly different from the general strokes illustrated. The key is just a guide to help you be able to visually pull apart the motifs and to understand what went into painting them. In most cases, the liner detail strokes are not included in the key as these can be variable, subject to whim. The three variations of the common crescent (illustrated on pages 8 and 9 as the "flat," "curved" and "sliding crescents" to denote their slight differences) are listed in the key generally as "crescent." The other, more distinctly different crescent varieties (elongated, ruffled, dipped) are each shown separately in the key.

Pictured below are a few of the basic strokes which will be illustrated in the pages that follow.

Broad stroke

Knife stroke

"S" stroke

Crescent stroke

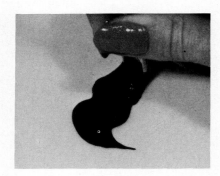

Dipped crescent

Comma stroke

Teardrop stroke

Fill-in swish

Chocolate chips

The photographs below show the steps involved in painting a circle stroke. Since retaining control of the brush to the finish of the circle stroke is usually very difficult, it's best to begin this stroke a little out of control—or in an awkward position—so that you will have greater control at the end. Note in figures 1 through 4 the changing positions of the fingers and brush as indicated by the rotation of the flag on the brush handle. Place a masking tape "flag" on your brush as a guide in following the illustration.

Fig. 1 Circle stroke, beginning

Fig. 2 Circle stroke, first quarter

Fig. 3 Circle stroke, first half

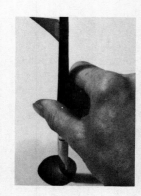

Fig. 4 Circle stroke, completed

Loading the Flat Brush and Basic Flat Brush Strokes

1. **Fully Loaded Brush**
   Load hairs completely and evenly, near or up to the metal ferrule.
2. **Dry Brush**
   On a paper towel wipe off nearly all paint. Use the dry brush to apply highlights.

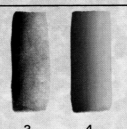

Whoops!

Here's what happens if insufficient care is taken in blending on the palette.

From these 2 strokes come all the strokes on these next three pages.

Knife   Broad

Knife Edged Stroke. Slide on the chisel edge of the brush, forming a thin, even line.
Broad Stroke. Press down the full width of the brush and pull with even pressure. End the stroke by standing brush perpendicular and lifting straight up, leaving a clean edge.

3. **Side-Loaded Brush**
   With moisture in the brush (water for acrylics and water colors, painting medium for oils) pick up color on one side of the brush. Blend on palette (in one spot, over and over) until color washes gradually across brush.
4. **Double-Loaded Brush**
   Two colors are picked up on opposite sides of the brush and palette blended until the transition from one color to another is smooth.

"S"

Begin on the knife edge. Slide. Gradually reverse directions and apply pressure, pulling a broad stroke. Gradually decrease pressure and reverse directions. Slide briefly on the knife edge. Slow down. Let brush hairs return to chisel edge. Stop. Lift off.

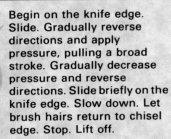

1   2   3   4   5

1. Beginning and ending are not the same length.
2. Stay in control at end; slow down. Let hairs return to chisel edge before lifting off.
3. Confusion about direction brush should go in. Draw some *ʃ* and paint over them.
4. Too much pressure in beginning. Slide on the chisel edge.
5. The ending curves too much.

Scroll

Begin on knife edge of brush. Slide upwards on the knife edge. Begin applying pressure as if painting a broad stroke. Curve gently around. Begin slowing down and releasing pressure. Stop. Let hairs return to chisel edge. Lift off.

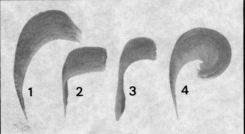

1   2   3   4

1. Fuzzy ending. Slow down. Stay in control.
2. Side too straight, curve too abrupt. Flow gradually.
3. Too much pressure in beginning. Slide on chisel edge.
4. Working too hard, rotating brush.

Flat Comma

This stroke is like the scroll stroke, only done in reverse direction; i.e. begin at fat end, slide to knife edge.

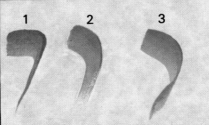

1   2   3

1. Too angular. Try to slide gradually from broad stroke into knife edge.
2. Lifting off too quickly. Slow down and stay in control.
3. Folding brush over on downward side.

Leaf Stroke

Begin as if to paint a broad stroke. Slowly begin pulling the stroke and rotating the brush simultaneously (by pulling the brush with your thumb) to a 90 degree angle. End by sliding briefly on the knife edge.

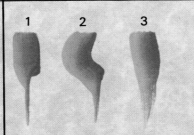

1   2   3

1. Too sudden a change from broad stroke to knife edge, and too rapid a decrease in pressure. All the movements should flow gradually together.
2. This stroke is curving out and around rather than rotating.
3. Keep those brush hairs in contact with painting surface until stroke is complete.

Flat Brush Strokes (cont'd)

Pivot/Pull

Begin as if to paint a broad stroke. Pivot in a quarter circle and gradually release pressure, sliding downward into a knife edge.

Whoops!

1 2 3

1. Brush swung out and around rather than pivoted, leaving a gap in the center. This stroke is used in making leaves (page 19).
2. Pressure was released too abruptly.
3. Stroke was begun with flat edge vertical (see line) rather than horizontal.

Bumpy Pivot/Pull

Form the stroke as above, only vary pressure and release to create "bumps." Nice for leaves (combine 2 strokes).

Whoops!

1 2 3

1,2,3. These are the same problems as listed above.

Half-a-Heart

Begin stroke at the line. Press upwards and rotate counterclockwise in half circle. Gradually release pressure while sliding on knife edge.

Whoops!

1 2 3

1. Pressure released too suddenly, causing an abrupt spike.
2. Stroke was swung out rather than pivoted, causing a gap in the center.
3. Half circle pivot was not completed. If using a double loaded brush (as shown) the color which is on top of the stroke should be the color which leads down to the point.

Corner Smash

Hold the brush as if to pull a knife stroke towards you. Press hard on the corner nearest you, causing the far corner to smash down as well. Begin pulling the stroke towards you, gradually releasing pressure.

Whoops!

1 2

1. Messy ending—caused by lifting off too rapidly and not letting hairs return to chisel edge. Also caused by a too wet or too tired brush which won't form a sharp chisel.
2. Pressure released too suddenly.

Flat Crescent

Think of windshield wipers. Rotate from 11 o'clock to 1 o'clock. Keep pressure even. Nice for adding flat petals around a circle.

Whoops!

1

1. You're working too hard here, forming a half circle. On a flower, this would cause too much overlapping of strokes; thus confusion. Keep it simple.

Curved Crescent

This stroke also rotates from 11 o'clock to 1 o'clock, but a little pressure is added in center, causing top to curve.

How nice—
Usually no problems with this one.

Note:
The flat and curved crescent and the sliding crescent (shown on next page) are all referred to throughout the book in the "Look For These Strokes" sections as "Crescent" to economize on space. Just be aware of the differences in forming the three crescents.

Flat Brush Strokes   (cont'd)

Sliding crescent

Begin, sliding very briefly on knife edge. Apply pressure as for a broad stroke, curving across top. Gradually release pressure, letting hairs return to chisel.

Whoops!

1   2   3

1. Flip-over on right (or left) side. Prevent this by keeping lead color (the one that slides up and over the top of the stroke) always to the outside edge.
2. Too square, too abrupt a pressure change.
3. Closes off too tightly at base.

Dipped Crescent

Form as above, but slow down near center of stroke, releasing pressure slightly, then reapplying it to form dip. Don't stop, just slow down.

Whoops!

1   2

1. Crease in center is caused by stopping in mid stroke while releasing pressure. Slow down, but don't stop!
2. Flip-over, a common problem. See Sliding Crescent.

Ruffled Crescent

Slide briefly on knife edge. This stroke is executed like the crescent, except that varying amounts of pressure are applied and released. End with a slight slide on knife edge.

Whoops!

1   2

1. Too square. Concentrate on gradual pressure change and curves instead of corners.
2. Ruffles too regular, too ridgy. Vary amount of pressure applied.

Elongated Crescent

Slide upwards on knife edge. Rotate brush across top in quarter turn applying pressure. Begin sliding downwards, rotating brush back into original position. Lead up with pink, down with red.

Whoops!

1   2

1. Gap is caused by not applying enough pressure and rotating. On the downward stroke, be sure edge of brush nearest you overlaps center of previously painted upward stroke.
2. Flip-over. See Sliding Crescent.

Straight Edged Crescent

Draw a line. Paint along it, keeping lower edge of brush on line with lots of pressure. Top of brush will fan upwards forming an arch. This is a good exercise to demonstrate effects of uneven pressure on brush.

Whoops!

1   2

1. Pressure must be applied unevenly to brush to paint straight and curved in one application. Pressure is even here. Try leaning handle of brush back towards you slightly.
2. Confusion of stroke—making half circles and sliding under the bottom.

Circle

Refer to step-by-step photos on page 6.

Whoops!

1   2

1. Uneven pressure (as illustrated in Straight Edged Crescent above) causes hairs of brush to splatter out over edge of circle.
2. Do-nut effect is caused by swinging out too far rather than pivoting on the brush. Also, note skipped areas where brush was too dry. Add more paint or water.

Liner Warm-Up Exercises

Dancers have stretching exercises, pianists have scales, singers have do-re-me's . . . Every activity, in which excellence is a goal, has its warm-ups and exercises. Often, many of the "kinks" can be worked out in these pre-performance exercises so the entire production can be carried off without a hitch.

This is also true of painting. The warm-up exercises on this page are good for limbering up shoulder/hand coordination as well as eye/hand coordination. Do them not only as a one-time drill to see how well you fare, but also every time you sit down to paint. They will help you develop a feel for the proper loading of your brush, the ideal paint consistency, the rhythm and flow of brush work, and the optimum pressure and release control.

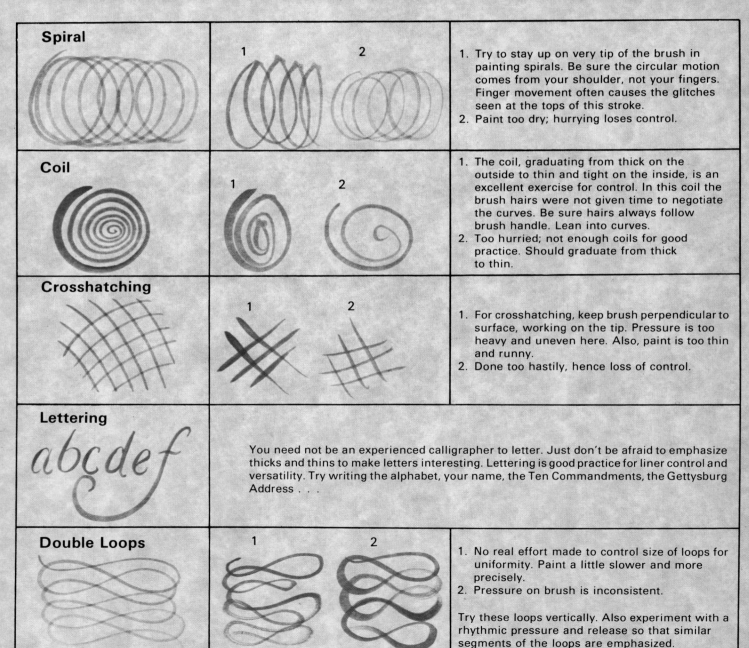

Do It Like This	Whoops!	What's Wrong
Spiral	1 2	1. Try to stay up on very tip of the brush in painting spirals. Be sure the circular motion comes from your shoulder, not your fingers. Finger movement often causes the glitches seen at the tops of this stroke. 2. Paint too dry; hurrying loses control.
Coil	1 2	1. The coil, graduating from thick on the outside to thin and tight on the inside, is an excellent exercise for control. In this coil the brush hairs were not given time to negotiate the curves. Be sure hairs always follow brush handle. Lean into curves. 2. Too hurried; not enough coils for good practice. Should graduate from thick to thin.
Crosshatching	1 2	1. For crosshatching, keep brush perpendicular to surface, working on the tip. Pressure is too heavy and uneven here. Also, paint is too thin and runny. 2. Done too hastily, hence loss of control.
Lettering *abcdef*	You need not be an experienced calligrapher to letter. Just don't be afraid to emphasize thicks and thins to make letters interesting. Lettering is good practice for liner control and versatility. Try writing the alphabet, your name, the Ten Commandments, the Gettysburg Address . . .	
Double Loops	1 2	1. No real effort made to control size of loops for uniformity. Paint a little slower and more precisely. 2. Pressure on brush is inconsistent. Try these loops vertically. Also experiment with a rhythmic pressure and release so that similar segments of the loops are emphasized.

Liner and Round Brush Strokes

Diamond

Begin on tip of brush. Pull towards you, slowly increasing pressure. At center, begin slowly decreasing pressure and pull to end.

Whoops!

1 2 3

1. Beginning and ending "tails" should be same length.
2. Pressure was applied and released suddenly. It should change gradually.
3. Too heavy handed at the beginning of the stroke. Stay up on tip of brush.

"S"

Use the same pressure and release process as for diamond, applying pressure as you reverse direction and then decreasing pressure as you reverse back.

Whoops!

1 2 3 4 5

1. Hooked on the bottom end. Make top and bottom match.
2. Sudden reverse of direction and application of pressure at top. Keep it gradual.
3. Same problem as "2", only at bottom.
4. Confusion over how many changes of direction should be involved (three).
5. Too "S-ie." Pull the curves out to a graceful flow. Save curves for scrolls.

Crescent

Begin on the tip. Follow process for diamond but instead of pulling a straight stroke, curve it around.

Whoops!

1 2 3

1. Closed in too much at base.
2. Too square, and pressure change a little too abrupt.
3. Ended too fast, out of control; leaves fussy ending.

Dipped Crescent

Same as above except dip in the center and apply heavy pressure and release; then continue to end.

Whoops!

1

1. Dip in center was abruptly done—with a stop and start motion. Try to have the dip thick but smooth.

Teardrop

Have plenty of paint in mid section of brush. Begin on tip. Pull and slowly apply pressure. Stop. Lift brush straight up.

Whoops!

1 2 3 4

1. Too heavy handed at the start. Stay on the tip. Glide down onto painting surface, being in motion when you touch down and **keep going**.
2. Come to a complete stop, then lift straight up to avoid a "pointy" head.
3. Apply pressure gradually, not all at once.
4. Avoid pushing back on the hairs in the process of lifting up the brush.

Pigtail Teardrop

Paint as for teardrop, but do not lift off brush at end. Stand it back up and drag a little wiggle through the fat part of the stroke.

Whoops!

1

1. Wiggly tail is too long; leaves some confusion as to which is the main tail.

Liner and Round Brush Strokes (cont'd)

Teardrop Push

Beginning on the tip of the brush, follow the directions for the teardrop stroke. Before lifting off at the end, push the brush slightly as if making a chocolate chip.

Whoops!

1

1. Beginning is a bit too thick. Start on the tip, then apply pressure steadily but gradually. Stop abruptly and flick the tip with a sideways push.

Comma

Press the brush down and pause, letting "head" round out. Gradually begin pulling the stroke and releasing pressure. Slow down, letting hairs return to point. Stop. Lift off. Practice large and small and streaked. See note to right.

Whoops!

1   2

1. This stroke was "pulled" before hairs had a chance to fan out. Remember to press and pause.
2. Too hurried at the end. Slow down to let hairs draw back to a point.

Note: Form a streaked comma by loading the brush with one color, then dipping just the tip in another color. Tap off excess on palette.

Wiggly Tail Comma

Begin making a comma stroke. As you release pressure, wiggle the "tail" of the stroke.

No "whoops" here. This is one you just can't ruin. It is used for making calyxes on rose buds and other buds. Works nicely, too, as a streaky stroke. See note, above right.

Chocolate Chip

Begin by pressing a blob. Flick the tip of brush through the blob.

Whoops!

1   2   3

1. So tiny. Be bold.
2. Tail is too long.
3. Too spikey.

Fill-In Swish

This one works best if you swish through it fast. Press the brush down (along line). Rotate brush so tip slides upwards. Then pull a comma stroke. See note at right.

Whoops!

1   2

1. Just a big chocolate chip in reverse. Be sure to rotate brush tip upwards.
2. Just a bent comma stroke. Slide the tip as above, and then pull tail through center of blob.

Note: Done with plenty of texture, this stroke resembles a turned leaf—often complete with veins. Keep it casual and spontaneous. I use it a lot in floral design.

Scroll

Whoops!

1

2

1. Stroke formed stiffly with fingers rather than from shoulder.
2. Line width shows no variation, no thick/thin. Very boring.

Doodling with the Liner

Rather than practice page after page of single brush strokes, you may as well have some creative fun while you build your skills.

Combine two or more strokes to form flowers, borders, ribbons, ferns . . . Relax. Just let your mind wander and your brush along with it. In almost no time you'll discover the joy of creating endless varieties of stroke combinations.

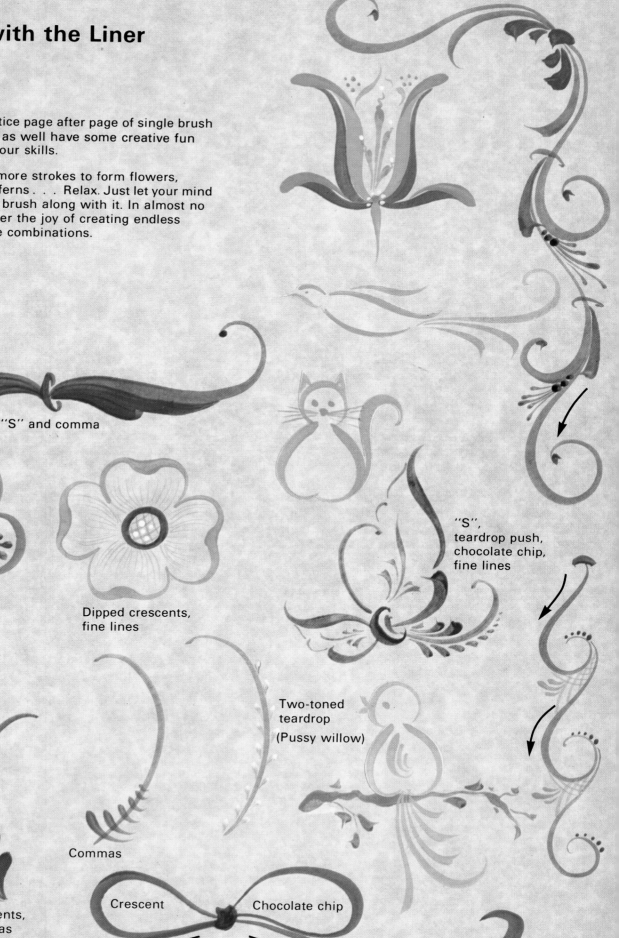

"S" and comma

Crescents, spiral, teardrops

Dipped crescents, fine lines

"S", teardrop push, chocolate chip, fine lines

Two-toned teardrop (Pussy willow)

Commas

Commas

Crescents, commas

Crescent

Chocolate chip

Scroll

Crosshatching

There is so much more to crosshatching than mere straight lines intersecting one another. Crosshatching can be used to create form and dimension. It can help convey a light, airy, delicate look as well as bold expressions to a decorative design.

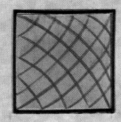

Note the different effects between straight and curved crosshatching lines.

Let's crosshatch some circles: First draw a circle and mark a cross inside it to use as guide lines.

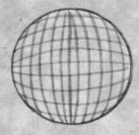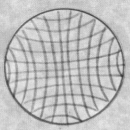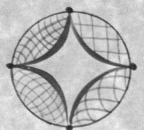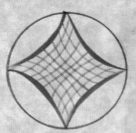

Note how lines converge toward center, following outside contours and making circle appear convex.

Here, the lines diverge from center making the circle appear concave.

Some ways to crosshatch the edges of a circle.

See how differently the interiors of these circles appear because of the differences in crosshatch direction.

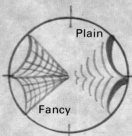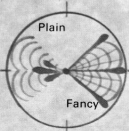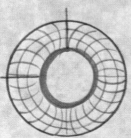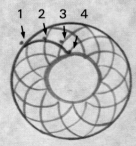

Follow contours, curving in towards the center.

Follow contours, curving outwards.

Crosshatch edges, following contours of comma strokes.

Begin this one by curving lines away from center vertical line and towards center horizontal line.

After curving lines in a spiral fashion in one direction, place intersecting lines in the opposite direction so they make contact with four o the curving lines.

Divide three circles above into 8 pie shapes to provide a guide for cross-hatching.

Crosshatch some scalloped edges:

1. Curve lines away from the center vertical line.
2. Each crossing line makes contact with previous lines.

1. Place one set of curved lines beginning just to the left of center line.
2. Place the crossing lines, beginning just to the right of center. Lines should intersect on the center vertical line.

1. Begin at the center vertical line and draw diagonal lines as illustrated.

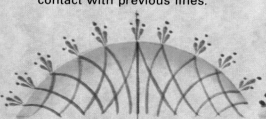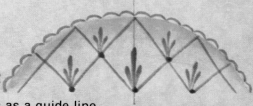

Draw a vertical line through the center of the scallops as a guide line.

Making evenly spaced crosshatching

1. Make an "X" connecting corners.

2. Paint diagonals, evenly spaced, first one direction,

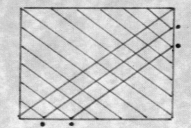

3. Then in the other direction, beginning and ending them on the same spot as previously painted diagonals for even spacing (see dots).

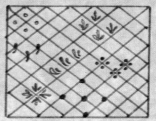

4. Finished section. Embellish with dots or strokes, or shade sides, or leave plain.

Base for a large flower

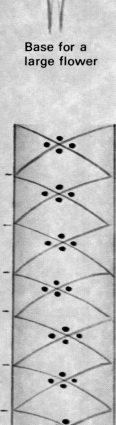

Mark length at 1/2" intervals. Draw a curved "X" in each 1/2" segment.

Try double lines.

Don't be afraid to experiment!

Mark length at 1/2" intervals. Draw "X's" spanning two segments.

What a difference a crosshatch pattern makes.

Have A Heart

How to make a heart:

1

a. Make a half circle counterclockwise.

b. Then gradually release pressure and slide to a point.

2

Repeat stroke on the other side reversing to a clockwise half circle. Overlap slightly to avoid a gap in the center.

Whoops!

A big gap in the center of the heart is caused by swinging out and too little pressure. Don't swing, pivot.

Fix it:

Use a smaller brush to paint another heart inside.

Outlining is caused by not rotating a full half circle.

Be sure that the edge of the brush which paints the top of the heart also paints the point at the base. **Rotate.**

Apply lots of pressure in the circle for a full rounded heart.

Look For These Strokes

Half-heart

Several years ago in Pennsylvania Dutch country, I learned how a true Penn. Dutch heart is made.

Draw 4 circles as shown. Trace around the outside edges of the top two, and along inside edges of the bottom two.

What's inside a heart?

What's on top a heart?

Have a Heart

What's around a heart?

Pssst. You could also put all this stuff inside the hearts.

Calico Red,
#10 flat

What's underneath a heart?

Calico Red,
Raspberry Wine
#10 flat

What hooks hearts together?

Raspberry Wine,
#6 flat

Rusty Nail,
#4 flat

Red clay,
#2 flat

Of course, hearts don't always have to be red.

You embellish
this group.

Bluegrass,
#6 flat

Ornamental Medallions

1984

Use medallions on
backs, bottoms, insides,
tops . . . of boxes and
other projects.

An imaginary fountain!

Shaw

Medallions can be a nice
finishing touch or
the central
design.

Love

On all designs, begin strokes at base and
pull them outwards just as if they were growing.

Leaves

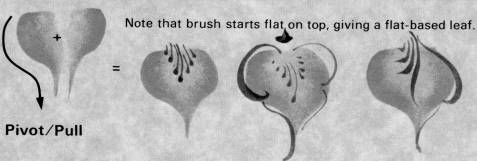

Look For These Strokes

| Leaf stroke | Pivot/ pull | Bumpy pivot/pull | Half-heart | Crescent | Flat comma |

Leaf Stroke

Do it hastily and get "quickie leaves."

Pivot/Pull

Note that brush starts flat on top, giving a flat-based leaf.

=

—ideal for tucking up against flowers to give the appearance of a leaf being attached **under** the flower, not **to** its petals.

Triple Stroke Leaf

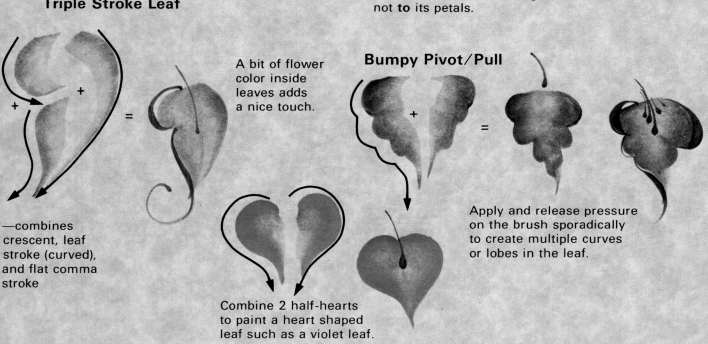

+
+
=

—combines crescent, leaf stroke (curved), and flat comma stroke

A bit of flower color inside leaves adds a nice touch.

Bumpy Pivot/Pull

+
=

Apply and release pressure on the brush sporadically to create multiple curves or lobes in the leaf.

Combine 2 half-hearts to paint a heart shaped leaf such as a violet leaf.

Whoops!

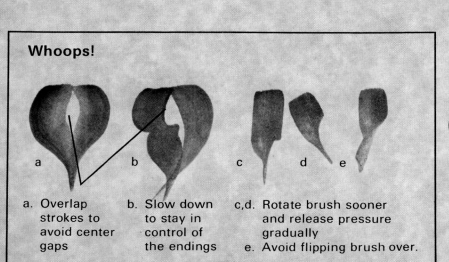

a.   b.   c.   d.   e.

a. Overlap strokes to avoid center gaps
b. Slow down to stay in control of the endings
c,d. Rotate brush sooner and release pressure gradually
e. Avoid flipping brush over.

Quadruple Stroke Leaf

—combines 2 crescents and 2 leaf strokes.

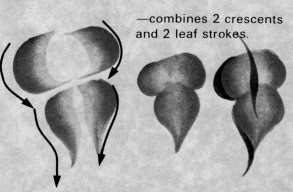

Leaves

Multi-lobed Leaf

Scroll

"S"

Pack these strokes closely together to make a multi-lobed leaf.

1   2
3   4
5
=

Look For These Strokes

Scroll   "S"   Leaf stroke   Crescent   Dipped crescent

Holly

Crescent

Leaf stroke

+   =

Be sure to overlap in center.

Pull brush with thumb (lefties push).

Push brush with thumb (lefties pull).

Combine leaves by butting one up against another.

Details

Shade "underneath" leaves with a side-loaded wash of dark color.

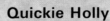

Quickie Holly

Dab, dab, dab dark green.

Then dab, dab light green

Add metallic gold details and red berries.

Dipped Crescent

Keep it open to tuck up against flower.

Close it on the bottom to stand apart from flower.

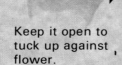

Leaves (cont'd)

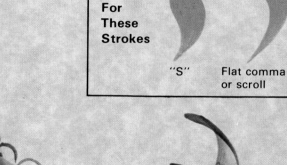

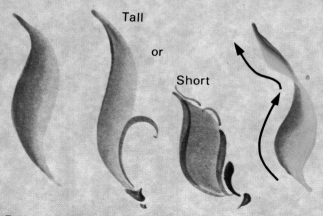

Tall

or

Short

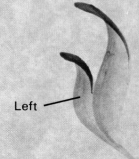

Right

Left

For many designs, a single "S", plain or embellished, makes a sufficient leaf.

Add a flip to the tip of this "S" leaf by leaning the brush to the right until you reach the dot, then lean to left.

Make an "S" double leaf by adding a shorter "S" to the right or to the left of a taller "S".

Combine 3 or more "S" strokes,

Whoops!

Be sure to overlap "S" strokes slightly to avoid unpleasant gaps.

Overlap

(Save the gaps for feathers)

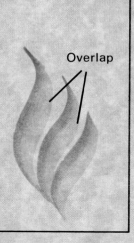

or

Try combining an "S" and a flat comma or scroll stroke.

Now put the flat comma or scroll stroke on the other side of the "S" for another interesting variation.

You will want to be able to paint these combinations in all directions, so grab another practice sheet and do it all again, this time reversing the "S" stroke to face the other way.

Leaves (cont'd)

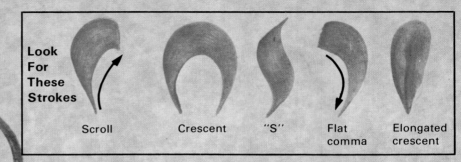

Look For These Strokes

Scroll   Crescent   "S"   Flat comma   Elongated crescent

A single or double scroll stroke suggests a graceful leaf.

Tuck the second and any succeeding strokes close to the first stroke. Avoid "gap-osis"

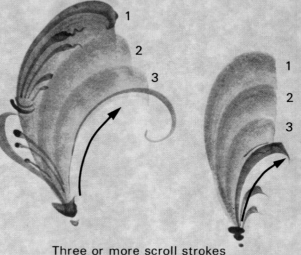

Three or more scroll strokes combined make a broad leaf. (Also ideal for bird tails and wings.)

Whoops!

Beware the "gap"!

Gaps are cumbersome and make detailing difficult

Dare to Doodle!

Combine the scroll, crescent, and flat comma for this stylized leaf. Begin with the outside layer and add as many layers inside as you like. Think of this formation as if you were walking up the stairs on the left (scroll strokes) across the landing (crescent stroke), and then down again on the other side (flat commas).

Fancy

Plain

Lefties, begin this leaf on the right with scroll strokes and end on left with flat commas.

Calyxes

—A few suggestions
for finishing off
the bottoms of
flowers.

**Look
For
These
Strokes**

← Flat →
brush

All strokes, except the 2 noted, were done with a liner.

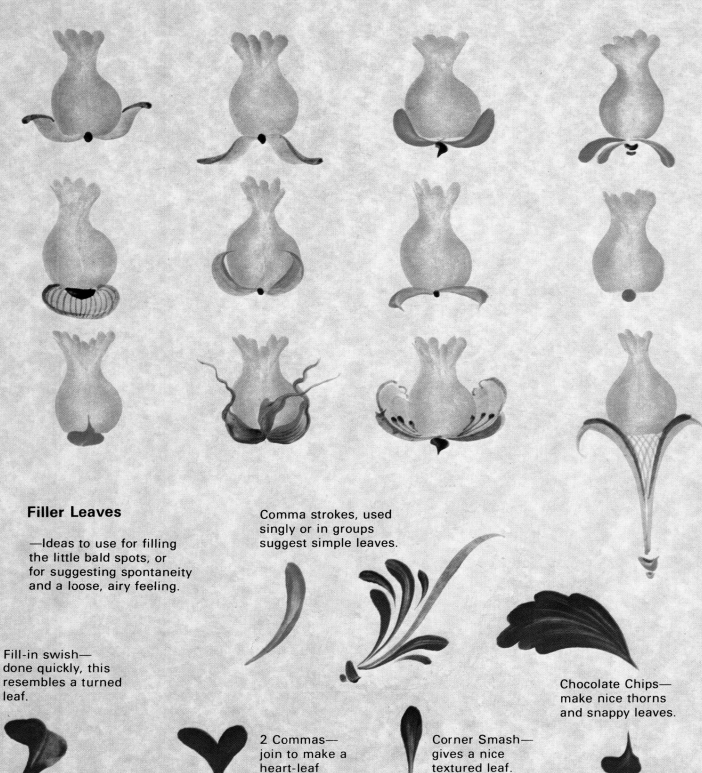

Filler Leaves

—Ideas to use for filling
the little bald spots, or
for suggesting spontaneity
and a loose, airy feeling.

Comma strokes, used
singly or in groups
suggest simple leaves.

Fill-in swish—
done quickly, this
resembles a turned
leaf.

2 Commas—
join to make a
heart-leaf

Corner Smash—
gives a nice
textured leaf.

Chocolate Chips—
make nice thorns
and snappy leaves.

Ball Flowers

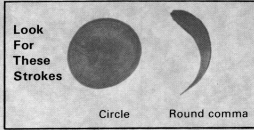

Look
For
These
Strokes

Circle   Round comma

Start with a ball.

Promenade

Raspberry Wine

Then begin adding
an abundance of
comma stroke petals.

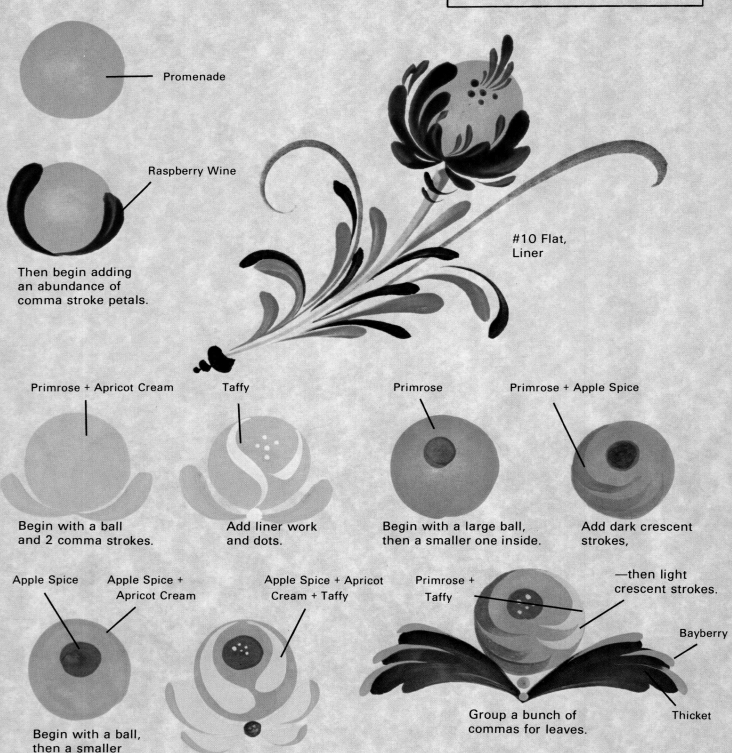

#10 Flat,
Liner

Primrose + Apricot Cream

Begin with a ball
and 2 comma strokes.

Taffy

Add liner work
and dots.

Primrose

Begin with a large ball,
then a smaller one inside.

Primrose + Apple Spice

Add dark crescent
strokes,

Apple Spice   Apple Spice +
Apricot Cream

Begin with a ball,
then a smaller
one inside.

Apple Spice + Apricot
Cream + Taffy

Add 2 large comma
strokes inside and
several smaller ones
outside. Detail with
small commas and dots.

Primrose +
Taffy

—then light
crescent strokes.

Bayberry

Thicket

Group a bunch of
commas for leaves.

Ball Flowers (cont'd)

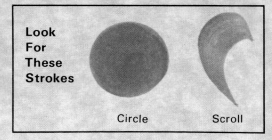

Look For These Strokes

Circle   Scroll

Use some of the symmetrical designs below as very stylized flowers or as center motifs on ring boxes, chipboard or Bentwood boxes, plates, circular trays, lazy susans, tilt top tables, clocks . . . Begin with the design in the center and build out from it with scrolls, flowers, crosshatching.

Numbers show painting sequence.

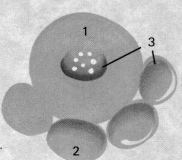

Shade the large and small balls with a sideloaded wash of color. Add detail strokes.

For all of the designs on this page, begin with a ball, then doodle with detail strokes.

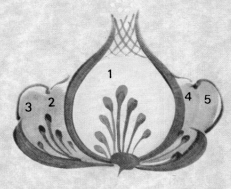

Brushes:
Flats #4,8,10
Jackie's Liner (JS-2)

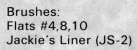

Several embellishing possibilities are illustrated on the ball flowers at left. Choose one combination, then carry out a complete design such as at right.

What could be easier than forming a circle flower with handle end of the brush. Add a few dots and comma stroke leaves and, presto—a border design!

Half-circle Flowers

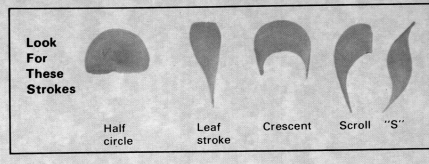

Look For These Strokes

Half circle   Leaf stroke   Crescent   Scroll   "S"

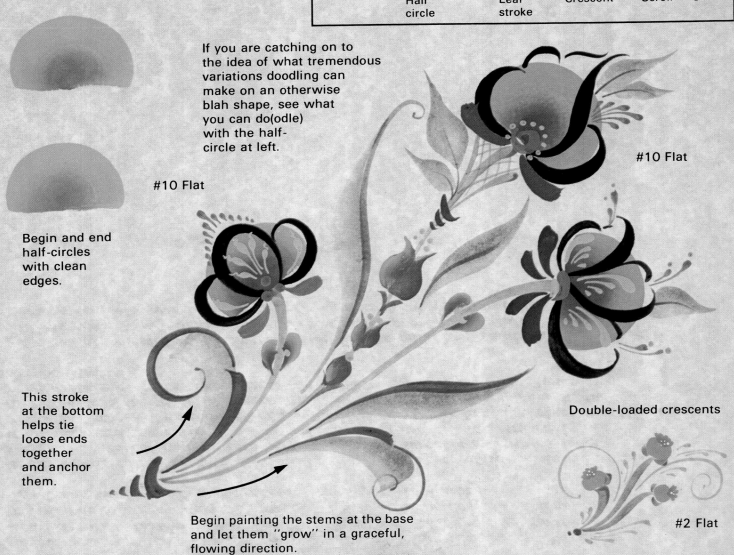

If you are catching on to the idea of what tremendous variations doodling can make on an otherwise blah shape, see what you can do(odle) with the half-circle at left.

#10 Flat

#10 Flat

#10 Flat

Begin and end half-circles with clean edges.

This stroke at the bottom helps tie loose ends together and anchor them.

Double-loaded crescents

Begin painting the stems at the base and let them "grow" in a graceful, flowing direction.

#2 Flat

How marvelously fun that three different flowers could grow on the same plant—where else but in a garden of imagination

Put together 2 half-circles (round on top),

or 2 quarter circles (flat on top).

Then add several small crescents.

#6 Flat

Teardrops

Dots outside

Dots inside

Crescent Flowers

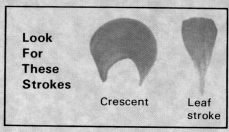

Look For These Strokes

Crescent

Leaf stroke

Now let's try some simple crescent stroke combinations.

Patchwork Green

Apple Spice

Taffy

Sunny Yellow

Taffy

Sunny Yellow

Raspberry Wine

Patchwork Green

#8 Flat

Clover

#2 Flat

Use assorted blues and pinks.

Paint flowers first, then leaves.

#8 Flat

Full face (crescent strokes are all the same size)

or

Facing upwards (crescent strokes in back must be flatter to take into consideration foreshortening)

Doodle, and do some ridiculous things. Remember, you're not trying to impress anyone; you're just having fun. And there's no telling what neat effect you may stumble onto.

How to do it:

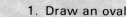
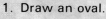
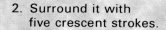

1. Draw an oval.

2. Surround it with five crescent strokes.

3. Paint leaf stroke in a line with center oval.

4. Paint center oval by double loading the brush.

5. Shade leaf stroke.

6. Add comma strokes, dots, and "S" stroke details if desired.

1

2   3

Follow the numbered sequence of strokes.

Filler flowers

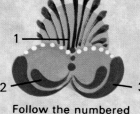

#2 Flat

Apple Spice

Apricot Cream

Crescent Flowers

(cont'd)

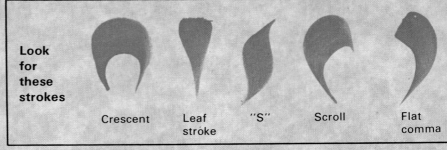

Look for these strokes

Crescent   Leaf stroke   "S"   Scroll   Flat comma

You can build exciting things out of **nothing** at all.

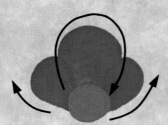

1. Start with "nothing."

2. Paint a crescent stroke then 2 scroll strokes, and finally a circle. Until the design gets dressed up, it can look pretty blah. Blahs are discouraging, so don't give up before dressing up.

3. Use the liner to give those basic strokes some pizzazz.

5. How about a threesome? Throw in a stem.

4. If one is good, 2 must be better. Repeat the design to make a double motif. Add some "leaves."

6. There are other things you can do with a "fourth" than just play bridge. See how the simple stroke combinations in step 2, above, can be turned into an elaborate design on the next page.

One thing leads to another and our "nothing" is soon obscured by embellishments as the design becomes more and more elaborate.

esigning Made Easy

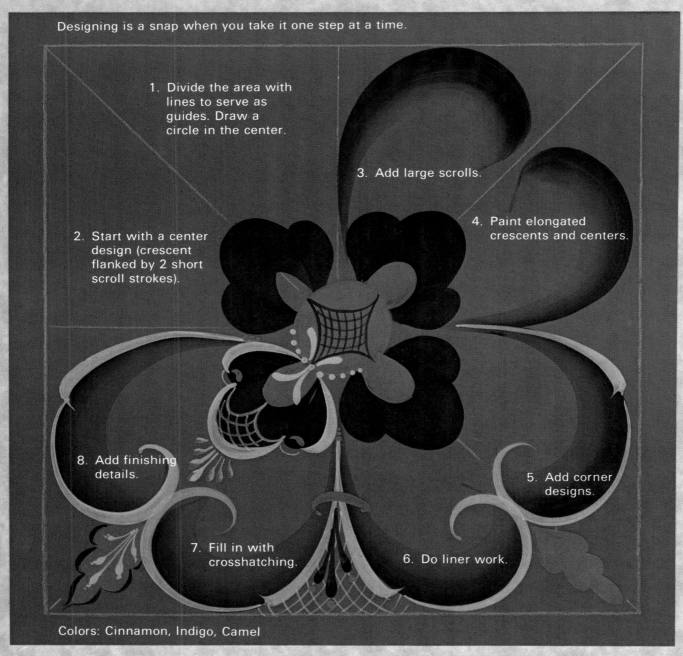

Designing is a snap when you take it one step at a time.

1. Divide the area with lines to serve as guides. Draw a circle in the center.

2. Start with a center design (crescent flanked by 2 short scroll strokes).

3. Add large scrolls.

4. Paint elongated crescents and centers.

5. Add corner designs.

6. Do liner work.

7. Fill in with crosshatching.

8. Add finishing details.

Colors: Cinnamon, Indigo, Camel

Now, you try it. Use a pencil to sketch a design from the center outwards in the first box.

In the second box, begin the design on the edges and work towards the center (I've given you a start).

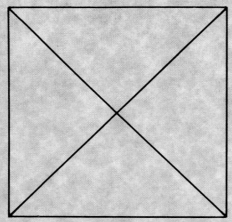

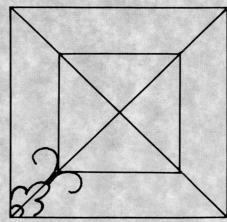

Crescent Flowers (cont'd)

Look For These Strokes

Crescent   Elongated crescent   Scroll   Flat comma

A 3/4" double-loaded brush (Rusty Nail and Harvest Gold) was used for this flower.

Detail work was done with Coffee Bean and Taffy

You decorate this one.

#10 Flat

The 3/4" brush was also used here.

Vary details. Emphasize thick and thin! Make your liner work exciting.

Paint three of these to create flower below

#12 and #8 flat brushes were side-loaded here. Harvest Gold petals were painted first, then the Rusty Nail ones.

All three segments of this flower have been embellished differently to give you more ideas. For consistency, all segments of your flower should be detailed identically.

Embellishing Details to Inspire You

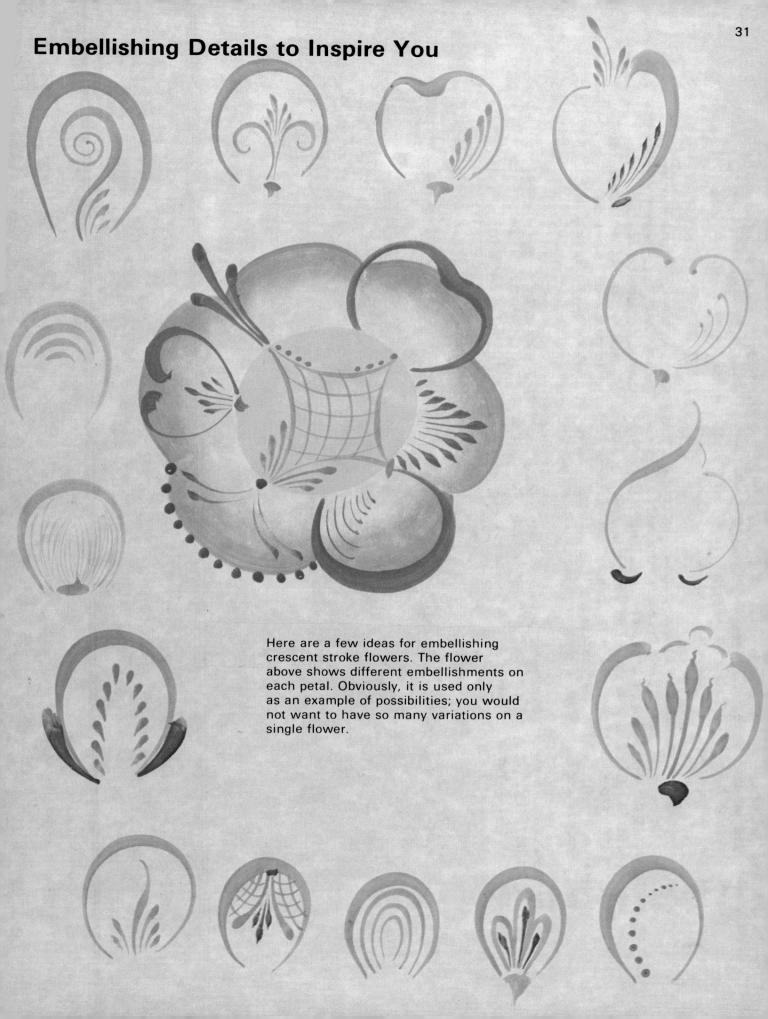

Here are a few ideas for embellishing crescent stroke flowers. The flower above shows different embellishments on each petal. Obviously, it is used only as an example of possibilities; you would not want to have so many variations on a single flower.

Elongated Crescents

Make a grouping of 3–5 elongated crescents.

Elongated crescent   Crescent   Scroll   Leaf stroke

Whoops!

Be sure to rotate brush sufficiently on downward stroke to overlap upward portion of stroke.

Follow the numbered sequence of strokes.

Combine 3 groups for a flower (brush was side-loaded here),

or

4 groups for a symmetrical flower or center motif (brush was double-loaded for this one).

Design a center motif

1. Begin with a cross

2. Paint 4 leaves

3. Add elongated crescents between leaves.

4. Embellish.

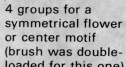
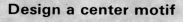

A Burst of Joy

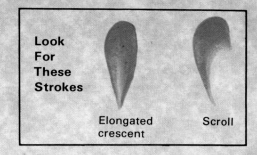
Just two different strokes and some liner detail work make it easy to create a fun fantasy flower.

Use a ½″ brush and paint big, bold and spiritedly. Don't worry about how it will turn out, just do it—and have fun while you do. Even if petals or leaves go astray, the result will look like it was great fun to paint.

Paint joyfully and it's certain that your joy will be reflected in your painting.

Labor, and others will appreciate and respect the labor; but missing will be the charm— pure and simple—of spontaneous creativity to express the joy of your heart.

NOTE: Many color suggestions have been included throughout this book. You may wish to try to duplicate some of the mixtures or combinations. It is important to remember, however, that the final printed page is several steps removed from the original artwork—(photography, developing, color separations, printing. . .). Many people, processes, chemicals, machines, inks, etc. have been involved in the process of full color printing. So even though you may be using the identical colors mentioned, your results may vary from the printed color. The important thing is to use colors and mixtures which please you.

Dipped Crescent Flowers

Let this stroke be casual so flowers do not appear too rigid.

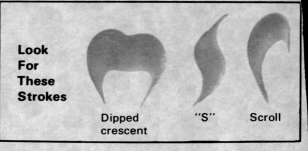

Look For These Strokes

Dipped crescent   "S"   Scroll

Sliding on the knife edge at beginning and ending of stroke leaves much empty space inside (room for another layer of petals).

Strong pressure but no slide flattens the bottom of the stroke.

Whoops!

Keep the leading edge of brush to outside edge of petal at all times to avoid "flip."

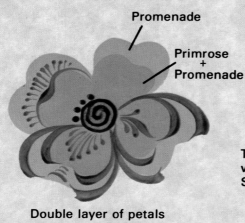

Promenade

Primrose + Promenade

Double layer of petals with assorted detailing.

Cotton Candy

Tinge the petal edges with color (Maple Sugar + Raspberry Wine),

or

Add liner detail strokes.

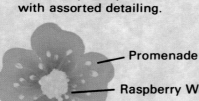

Promenade

Raspberry Wine

Use five petals to suggest a wild rose.

Cotton Candy

The smallest petals are merely dabs made with the corner of the brush.

Your first attempts on this flower are apt to be stiff.

Loosen up and let this be floppy.

2

1

Primrose

Raspberry Wine

Stack two dipped crescents in order shown. Add calyx.

Turn the double stack upside down and hang for droopy flowers.

Primrose

Promenade

Begin here

Stack many of the dipped crescents beginning with the largest at the base and growing ever smaller

uffled Crescents

Combine 4 or 5 ruffled crescents to form a delicate flower. #8 Flat.

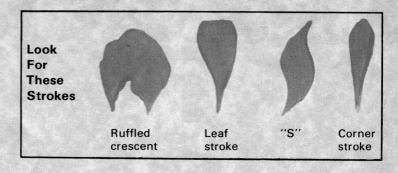

	Ruffled crescent	Leaf stroke	"S"	Corner stroke
Look For These Strokes				

Violets or Johnny Jump-Ups

#8 flat

1. Pivot a ruffled crescent.
2. Add four leaf strokes.
3. Paint yellow "hairs" and red dot.
4. Add fine liner details.

Colors used in the violets: Plum Pudding, Indigo, Cotton Candy, Buttercup, Calico Red.

Easy Stroke Iris

1. Paint large ruffled crescent. Double-load #10 flat.
2. Add 2 side petals.

Apricot Cream

Raspberry Wine + Bavarian Blue

Optional

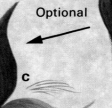

Slide the ruffled crescent, rotating brush as for elongated crescent.

Use some of iris color plus Heather and Cotton Candy, #8 flat.

c

a

b

3. Paint 2 "S" strokes, then 1 leaf stroke down into center of large petal.

4. Add 3 tall "S" strokes (optional—substitute corner stroke), Indigo + Raspberry Wine.

5. Add details:

a. "Ratty brush" yellow, then white.
b. Dark veins in ruffled crescents.
c. Dark veins on strokes from step 3.

Use 1/2" and #10 flat on large iris.

Some color mixtures to try:

Raspberry Wine + Plum Pudding
Raspberry Wine + Bavarian Blue
Promenade + Heather
Primrose + Heather
Apple Spice + Slate + Raspberry Wine + Heather

Plum Pudding + Indigo
Promenade + Indigo
Promenade + Bavarian Blue

To any of the above mixtures, add Taffy, Heather, or Wicker White.

Ruffled Crescents (cont'd)

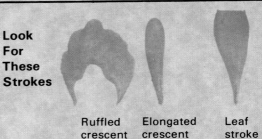
Easy Stroke Peonies

Use 5 values of color to paint the peonies with ruffled crescents.

Draw an oval.

1. Darkest value (Raspberry Wine), #10 flat

2. Dark value (Apple Spice + Calico Red + Primrose), #10 flat

3. Medium value (Primrose), #10 flat

4. Light value (Promenade + Primrose), #8 flat

5. Lightest values (Promenade, then Cotton Candy), #8 flat. Add Sunny Yellow dots.

To paint a zinnia or dahlia, follow the same steps as for the peonies, but paint regular crescents rather than ruffled ones.

Paint a chrysanthemum by placing regular crescents more loosely.

Easy Stroke Marigolds

Stem— leaf stroke, double-loaded #8 flat

Add 2 ruffled crescents, double-load #8 flat with Rusty Nail and Sunny Yellow.

Add 3 more petals.

Add 2–4 more smaller petals.

Add stamen with liner and Sunny Yellow and Rusty Nail. Add Lemonade dots.

Leaves consist of many elongated crescents.

Easy Stroke Daffodils

1. Slide upwards, then back down.

2. Fill in gap with dark value.

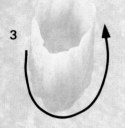

3. Slide a long way and then back up to elongate this stroke. Apply lots of pressure. Begin and end in same positions as step 1.

Turn the flower to face toward you by painting the base petals first and in a complete ring. Note: paint a stamen filled center in step 1 and you'll have a clematis.

Look For These Strokes

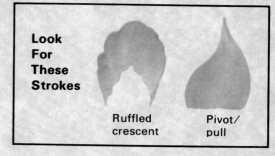

Ruffled crescent

Pivot/pull

Overlap petals as shown.

Paint petals marked "a" first, then paint petals marked "b."

#10 Flat

1. Paint petals with double-loaded brush, Lemonade, Sunny Yellow + Harvest Gold.

2. Paint center Harvest Gold.

3. Add small crescents around center.

4. Paint Persimmon in center.

5. Add yellow stamen.

Add ruffled crescents, pivot/pull, or bumpy pivot/pull at the base.

#8 Flat

Flip brush here.

6. Double-load a #4 flat brush to paint leaves Patchwork Thicket.

Paint flipped portion light.

Paint this section dark.

38

Scroll Flowers

Work from the outside towards the center.

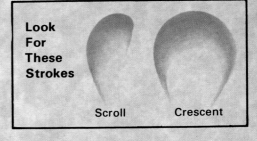

Look For These Strokes

Scroll   Crescent

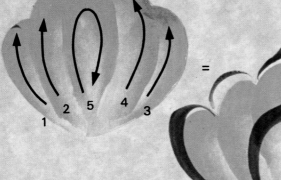

2 5 4 3
1

=

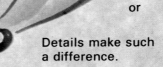

or

Details make such a difference.

Leave some air space within your liner work. It provides breathing room.

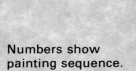

Numbers show painting sequence.

"Grow" from the base of the design outwards.

Use a large brush and a sideloaded wash of color. Work boldly—it helps to loosen you up.

croll Flowers

Lay a piece of tracing paper on this page and paint over the detailing and outline strokes to develop a feel for the flow of the embellishment.

Work your strokes in the same direction as the petals would grow—from the base outwards.

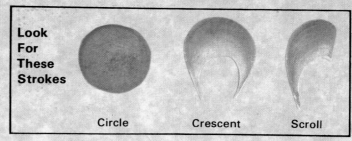

Look For These Strokes

Circle   Crescent   Scroll

Progression of strokes

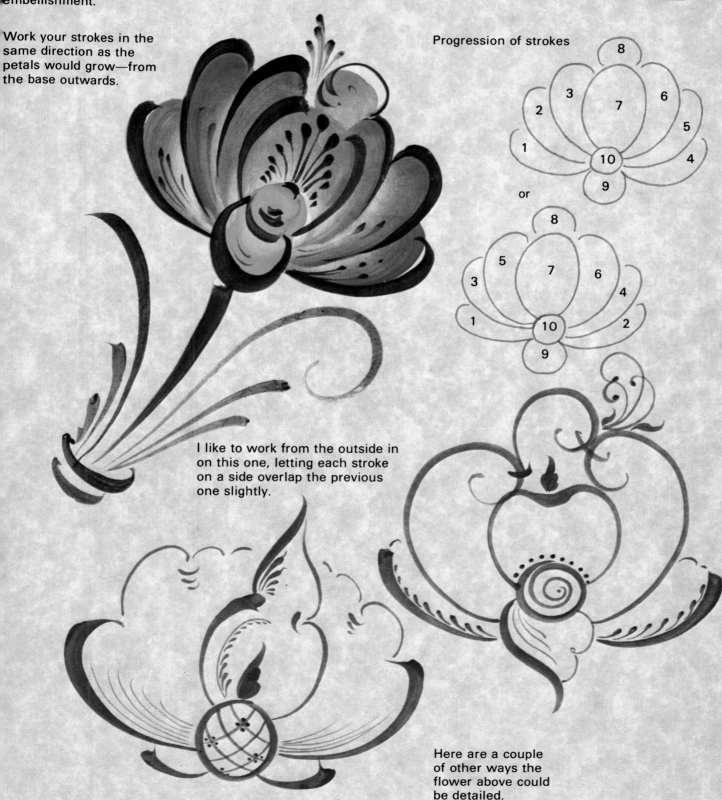

or

I like to work from the outside in on this one, letting each stroke on a side overlap the previous one slightly.

Here are a couple of other ways the flower above could be detailed.

Leaf Stroke Flowers

Load the brush with plenty of paint to provide texture. Make a dot to indicate flower center. Pull petal strokes toward the center.

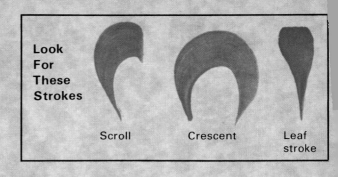

Look For These Strokes

Scroll   Crescent   Leaf stroke

Overlap some strokes or make some lean in the opposite direction to prevent a spiral effect.

Shorten petals in the back and flatten flower center to an oval shape to make the flower "look" up.

Add some color variation to the petals by loading the brush first with one color, then, after wiping the tip of the brush slightly on a paper towel, pick up a small amount of a second color.

For a variation— pull the stroke from the center out.

These leaves are also leaf strokes.

Add a second layer of petals in a slightly lighter value.

Harvest Gol Calico Red, #4 flat

For a quick bud, group 2 or 3 petals and hold together with a calyx (see page 23 for some possibilities).

Buttercup, Lemonde

Pivot/Pull Petals

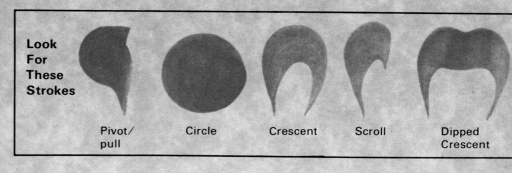

Look For These Strokes

Pivot/ pull　　Circle　　Crescent　　Scroll　　Dipped Crescent

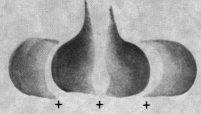

+　+　+

It all adds up to:

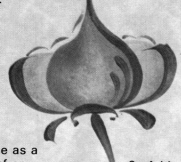

Use as a leaf or flower.

Start with a circle

Follow steps 1–3 for blue flower below. Then add dipped crescent center.

Use a double-loaded brush.

+　+

3. Paint fine lines.

2. Add center vein.

2　3

1

4

1. Paint the 2-stroke petal.

4. Paint crescent strokes center— back ones first, then front one.

1. Draw a center.
2,3. Paint 2-stroke petal.
4. Paint center.

Each petal has been embellished differently to give you lots of ideas.

Other ways to doodle on the petals.

Paint this one red for a stylized poinsettia.

Trumpet Flowers

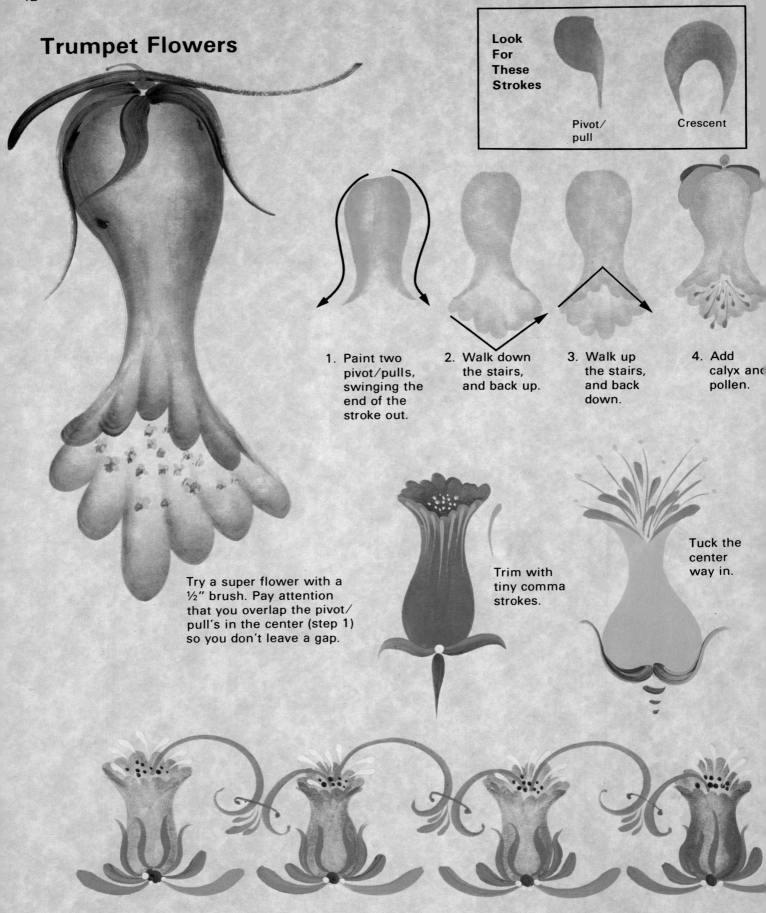

Look
For
These
Strokes

Pivot/
pull

Crescent

1. Paint two pivot/pulls, swinging the end of the stroke out.

2. Walk down the stairs, and back up.

3. Walk up the stairs, and back down.

4. Add calyx and pollen.

Try a super flower with a ½″ brush. Pay attention that you overlap the pivot/pull's in the center (step 1) so you don't leave a gap.

Trim with tiny comma strokes.

Tuck the center way in.

imple Little Flowers

Use these little flowers for quick decorations, or in combination with border designs.

Round comma

Corner smash

"S"

Crescent

Wicker White

+

+

=

#2 Flat

Primrose
Raspberry Wine

Optional—
shade white
with
Barnwood.

Corner stroke—
use lots of paint
for heavy texture.

Single
stroke
petals,

or

Double
stroke
petals.

Use tiny comma or
teardrop strokes
for this one.

Pencil eraser
(leaves a more
pronounced ring
than cotton
swab).

Place dots
at the tips
of petals
for variety.

This "ratty brush" flower, below, serves nicely to fill empty spaces in a floral arrangement and to soften a design. A ratty brush is a must. After ruining a round brush, give it to a youngster for a few months. Then reclaim it. It must be in wretched condition. Dance the brush through the paint, then onto the palette until most of the paint is removed. Then pounce the brush on your project, stippling a delicate flower. Three colors were used here.

Cotton swab flowers

"S" Stroke Tulips

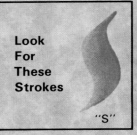

Look
For
These
Strokes

"S"

The tulips on these next 3 pages are based on "S" strokes. If you have difficulty making "S" strokes in one direction, do your weakest stroke first, then match the other side to it. If you have difficulty painting "S" strokes in either direction, go back to the exercises on page 7 and practice.

Generally, it works best for right handed painters to paint the left side first then the right. Left handed painters should begin with the right side, then do the left. In this way, it is possible to see the work already done when proceeding with the second step.

The tulips illustrated on these next pages were all painted with flat brushes. If you prefer, however, round brush "S" strokes work equally well.

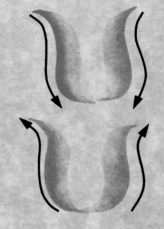

Pull strokes towards you to the base of the tulip.

Or, pull strokes away from the base.

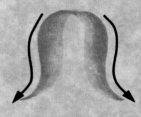

Some painters find it easier to pai their tulips upside down.

Let's begin with simple tulips:

Paint 2 "S" strokes.

Find the direction which suits you best; however, as always, it is a good idea to try to perfect your sk in painting strokes in all direction

Don't worry if you have fuzzy edg overlapping strokes. Embellishing details will minimize these problem

Then paint 2 more "S" strokes outside.

Add details.

Or, paint 2 more "S" strokes inside.

Add details.

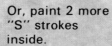

These tulips were done with a #10 flat and a side-loaded wash of Primrose. Details are Raspberry Wine + Primros

Tulips (cont'd)

Try 2 "S" strokes, tall and skinny

or,

short and fat, with an "S" in the middle,

or a crescent stroke,

or two pivot/pulls.

Look For These Strokes

"S" Crescent Dipped crescent Scroll Pivot/pull

Add cross-hatching.

Colors used on this page include:
Summer Sky
Robin's Egg
Bluegrass
Indigo
Wicker White
Clover
Coffeebean

Outline an open area and fill with dots.

Add dipped crescents on top of the "S" strokes.

Tulips (cont'd)

It's fun to unleash
your imagination and
see what happens.
Just remember—
there are no
prescribed
rules, so
anything
goes!

**Look
For
These
Strokes**

"S"   Scroll   Leaf
stroke   Pivot/
pull

Apple Spice

Pivot/pull + crescent

Rusty Nail

Harvest Gold

Cotton Candy

Promenade

Primrose

Some of these tulips were painted
with a side-loaded wash, others
were done with a double-loaded
brush. You should be able to tell
the difference.

Raspberry Wine

Plum Pudding

Promenade + Primrose

Cotton Candy

Calico Red

Persimmon

Thicket

Clover

Sunny Yellow

Harvest Gold

Autumn Leaves